The First Year And Day For Beginning Wicca

The First Year And Day For Beginning Wicca

A Guided Study Workbook For The Novice

By Nicci Zalliski

Copyright © 2017 by Nici Zalliski

All rights reserved. No part of this publication may be reproduced, distributed, or transmitted in any form or by any means, including photocopying, recording, or other electronic or mechanical methods, without the prior written permission of the publisher, except in the case of brief quotations embodied in critical reviews and certain other noncommercial uses permitted by copyright law. For permission requests, write to the publisher, addressed "Attention: Permissions Coordinator," at the address below.

Nici Zalliski
P.O. Box 1734
Clintwood, VA 24228
Or E-Mail requests to
zalliski@gmail.com

"Where once I prayed for forgiveness from a father God who held up huge palms and said "Thou shalt not," now I find peace with a sister god who takes my open hands in hers and says, "You will."
— Betsy Cornwell

TABLE OF CONTENTS

Introduction	6
What Is Wicca?	7
Definitions	17
A Brief History	20
Just A Few Traditions	24
Your First Steps	26
The Wheel Of The Year	29
Understanding The Basic Tenet's	33
Reviewing The Basic Tenet's	43
Final Thoughts	51

INTRODUCTION

First let me say Thank you for purchasing and reading this book. Whether you are new to Wicca, or looking for information, this workbook will give you a foundation of information, exercises, and research instructions for finding the knowledge you seek.

Honestly, I could have written out an informative book rather than allow you, the reader, to find the information yourself. However, the purpose of this workbook is to give you the clues to look for. There are many books on the market that explain at least some of the information you will gain from following the exercises and research assignments in this book. However, there isn't a single publication that provides all of what you will find here. In addition, by following the exercises and research assignments you, the novice, will gain a stronger foundation and smarter sense of what Wicca is and what it will mean to you.

It would be no good for me to simply tell you what Wicca is and what it should be for you. My definition for what Wicca should be for you may not fit you. In this way, you will have a better chance of succeeding in your search for whatever you're looking for in your Year and a Day of study in Wicca.

WHAT IS WICCA?

What is Wicca? Well, if you type in an internet search of this question you will likely find an answer similar to this: "A form of modern paganism claiming its origins in pre-Christian religions." You will also find a Catholic apologetic web page dedicated to diminishing Wicca as a whole.

Allow me to answer in my way. Wicca is an earth based religion which has its roots in the general belief that everything is connected. It fosters free thought and free will, encourages learning and understanding of the earth and her cycles, and affirms divinity in all living things. Wiccans observe the changes of the seasons, the phases of the moon, and the cycles of the sun. We reflect inwardly in search of finding the cycles within ourselves that correspond to those of the natural world, and we try to live in harmony with what we find. We live by the Law of Three and pay heed to the Wiccan Rede because these basic tenants teach us that all actions have consequences, and when those actions are ours then the consequences are ours as well.

Wicca and Witchcraft are two completely separate things. Wicca is the belief system, and the way of life. Witchcraft is our work, or spells, done. It's a little difficult at the beginning to see the true difference between the two, but as you continue your studies you will begin to see and feel the difference.

Wicca is not the stereo-type. We Wiccans do not bow down to, nor worship, Satan or any connected demons or monsters of Christian creation. Any and all bad or evil in the world was created by the people that were in the midst of it. If someone sees devil worship in what we do, then it's the person's mind that created such a distinction. In other words, the devil they see is one of their own making. Witchcraft is not the use of supernatural powers to hex, or harm others. For the past few centuries, the image of the Witch has been associated with evil, heathenism, and unrighteousness. Regardless of the origin of these misconceptions, they are exactly that and nothing more: Misconceptions.

Wicca has no central authority to punish heretics, and no dogma that can be used as a measuring stick to find people wanting as an excuse to torcher, harm, and kill nonbelievers. Witchcraft is not evil, and by nature, cannot be innately so. The consequences of a Witch's ritual may have a negative impact on someone or something, but you can bet that the witch will get smacked by the Law of Three later.

The Law of Three is an absolute, but it's not a tool to scare initiates or neophytes. It's simply a truth. Let me give you an example.

When I was 19 I cast a series of spells that had consequences for the preceding six years.

1.) I had a boyfriend, Todd, who had enlisted in the Marine Corps and he was stationed in another time zone. I cast a love spell to keep his heart
2.) My mother and her third husband had been married for three years. He was abusive. He used to say; "If I had a way to make money while being waited on hand and foot, I'd be doing that." He would say this because he didn't want to work. He would leave the house early in the morning around 5:00 a.m. and return after the rest of the household had left for work and school. I lived at home at 19. I was going to school, and I was too scared to leave my mom, and baby brother in that house alone with that man because I was the only one who could stand up to him.
3.) I'll get to later.

Basically, here's what happened. My boyfriend started to cheat on me with a girl who had grown up near where he was stationed. I cast another spell to force him to end the affair. We were, after all, making plans to get married when he came home on leave, and for me to move onto post with him. The affair with the other girl ended, and I flew up to visit him to seal the end of his 'affair' (as I saw it). That's when the main problem occurred. Upon seeing him, I suddenly realized that I no longer had substantial feelings for the man in front of me. I stayed for my visit, and went home after the three planned days. When I returned home I released him and myself from that spell, and called him to break up with him. He agreed about the breakup but he was so angry with me, without really understanding why. To this day he still doesn't know that I'm a Wiccan. After a period of about six years we started talking again, finally able to move on from what happened. I learned that he married the girl that he'd had an 'affair' with, and now has two beautiful children as a result of that marriage. Most importantly, they're still happily married more than ten years later.

I realize this may sound like a simple break-up, but it's not as easy as that. When a love spell is cast, that spell binds the people on both ends: the Witch who cast the spell, and the target of affection. The release of a love spell, depending on the spell, can be violent. It can create feelings of being hurt, but you don't know where it's coming from, and this is especially true for the target of affection if they don't know about the spell to begin with. If a love spell is cast, and never released, it can cause a different type of crisis. If the Witch and target are not compatible but the Witch is too delusional to see this, he or she can cause serious harm to his or her target if she keeps that person forever entangled in a love spell.

As much as I loved Todd, I had no right to bind him to me in that way. I had not right to interfere in his live. Granted- he shouldn't have cheated on me. He should have broken up with me and moved on. This is still no excuse for my actions. His heart was not mine, and it certainly wasn't mine to take. Although he was relieved about the break-up, the destructive effects of my spell made him angry. Like I said, Todd didn't understand why he was so angry with me. He only knew that he should be.

What I thought was an act of love that originated from the heart ended up being a source of real turmoil for him, and for me. It fractured our relationship, and us. My intentions may have been good, but the resulting effect created negative consequences for me to deal with.

The second spell was much more direct. You see, I cast a spell to give my step-father what he wanted: A way to have money while not working so that he could live to be waited on hand and foot. I cast these two spells, the love spell previously mentioned and this one, within the same lunar month. I had thought that if my step-father got what he really wanted then he would stop hurting my mother, and I could leave home without worrying that he would slaughter my mother and baby brother in one of his fits of rage. Needless to say, this is not what happened because three weeks later, he was hit by a dump truck.

To be more specific, he was drinking while driving his Ford Ranger. He crested the top of a hill while a dump truck was turning left into construction zone. If it still hasn't hit, that's a small truck that ran up underneath the front end of a dump truck while the dump truck's driver was legally crossing lanes of traffic to enter his place of work. My step-father was rushed to the hospital. The one factor that kept him from becoming a vegetable, according to the neurologists, was the fact that he is left handed. When we went to the junk yard to take pictures of the Ford Ranger for insurance, my little three year old cousin tried to climb into the driver's seat, but didn't fit. My step-father was 6'5" and weighed in excess of 250 pounds.

In the end, he got his wish. He got a large settlement, and lots of people to wait hand and foot on him. He lost function of the left side of his body, and spent two years in rehab re-learning how to walk, write, bathe, communicate, and basically function.

Eventually, he regained enough mobility to use his electric wheel chair to pin my mother against a wall so he could repeatedly beat her with his walking cane. He could walk, but he still used a chair around the house, and while shopping. Despite being physically handicapped, he had proven that he was still capable of beating my mom, and baby brother in fits of rage.

I cast my third spell. This time, after having seen the consequence of the two previously mentioned, I changed tack. I cast a spell to release my family of any ties to that man. Soon after, his sister filed for divorce from my mom on his behalf. He got everything. The house and land were his, but my mother and brother had their freedom from him. Now my mom is living in her own place making a living as an artist, and my baby brother just graduated with his Bachelors in Art. She's dating again, and I was finally able to move away and live my own life without worrying so much about them. But, for six years I tangled with the consequences of those spells.

Ever Mind the Rule of Three

Three Times Your Acts Return To Thee

This Lesson Well Thou Must Learn

Thou Only Gets What Thee Dost Earn.

This isn't a threat. This is a fact, and it's a reminder that what you put out is what you get back. When a Witch casts a spell she should do so with the full understanding that her intentions are as important as the final consequences whether the two are complementary or not. What actually happens as a result of your actions will boomerang back, bigger and with more force.

On the other hand, if you cast a spell with good intentions, and it turns out bad, keep in mind that in most cases you should be alright. Eventually it will pass, and you can move on. This isn't a threat of eternal pain. Remember also, that what doesn't kill you will make you stronger and wiser. Wicca is about learning, and understanding. If you make a mistake, you will pay for it, but you will also learn from it and know how to do it better next time.

Exercise 1

Before moving forward, take the time to complete this exercise. This should not be a short exercise. It should require considered and deliberate thought. Find a quiet place, settle your mind, and complete this exercise. You will need a few pieces of loose paper (or a notebook), a pen and relaxing music. Don't try to complete this exercise in one setting. You likely have other responsibilities. Start it and get as far as you can. Once you become frustrated, rather than skip ahead, put this book down and tend to your life. Come back to it once you can put your mind back into the proper frame for this exercise and finish at your own pace. Most importantly- Finish This Exercise <u>before</u> Moving Forward.

Objective: The purpose of this exercise is to get you to honestly asses your personal motivations, and ability to accept responsibility for your actions. Remember that the basic tenet is "Harm none."

Answer in full sentences. The answers you are looking for here are straightforward, without malice, and without blame. As Wiccans, we strive to find our best selves. As Witches we accept the consequences of our actions without blaming others. Period.

Question 1.1

Think back and remember a time when someone did something to you, and you reacted.

What was your response? Answer honestly and without qualifiers.

For example: One time my baby brother popped the heads off of my Barbie's, and then flushed the heads down the toilet. I responded to by brothers actions by slapping him in the face, and shoving his head into the toilet.

An improper answer would be that <u>because my brother was a brat and flushed the Barbie heads down the toilet I hit him, and put his head in the toilet and he deserved it. I was a child, and responded with childish emotions.</u>

Answer honestly without justifying your response. Own your past actions and accept them. Remember that a good reason is still only a great excuse.

Question1. 2

What were the ensuing consequences of your actions?

Example: In response to our fight, my grand-mother spanked me.

Inappropriate answer: My grand-mother should have also spanked my brother.

Question 1.3

Would you change anything from this incident if you could?

Question 1.4

Now remember a time when you didn't take action but you could have?

Did you survive?

Given your answers, is a reaction or response Always warranted?

Question 1.5

Name three positive influences in your life.

How have these influences shaped you?

Give 1,000- 1,500 words.

Question 1.6

Consider one memorable event in your life that helped to shape you into the person you are today.

What was the event?

How did it shape you? Give 1,000 words.

Question 1.7

Consider your motivations for walking the Wiccan Path.

What are you looking for?

What are you missing?

What first brought you to Wicca?

Exercise 2

Objective: The purpose of this exercise is to introduce you to the concept of Meditation, and forming a habit of practicing every day. Meditation is required to be able to ground, and charge- both of these abilities are needed for successful, and controlled spell work. Without meditation, your spells will either not work, or blow up in your face.

Meditation

That's right. I just said the horrible "M" word... Let me guess. You have no time for meditating. Your schedule is cram packed. You've got school, or work that you're already getting up before dawn for. Afterwards there is the spouse, kids, or other various responsibilities. Don't sweat this so much.

For such an important part of this path, this is probably the easiest thing to do. Really! I promise. It's much simpler than you are allowing yourself to believe. All you need is 1-5 minutes of alone time. When you take a shower do you take a quick 3 minute shower, or a 15 minute shower? Take two minutes under the running water to meditate. What about in your car? Of course I'm not suggesting you do this while driving. When you get to work sit in your car for an extra four minutes, if you're not in a rush to clock-in. Lunch time! Sure, schoolmates might find you meditating in the cafeteria hard to swallow, and they may think you're strange, but the thing about large groups of people is that once they're accustomed to something happening, it becomes the norm for them. At night just before bed.... Go to bed a few minutes before your normal bed time to sit quietly. What if the kids don't leave you alone? As I said before, once people are accustomed to an action, they stop questioning it. It is possible to get a 6 month old, a 3 year old, and an eight year old to sit quietly with their mother for two minutes- even if that's all you get. The more they acclimate to this habit, the longer they'll allow you to sit quietly by sitting with you. A by-product could be that you pass this great habit onto them. It's rare for children to proactively meditate, but it's a seed to plant that's been known to grow.

Finding time to meditate is the easy part. Often we balk and say that it's too difficult but that's because somewhere in our minds we're making excuses to ignore this discipline. Also, if you don't have time to meditate, you don't have time to practice the craft. Meditation is the foundation on which every work you will ever complete is built. Your ability to meditate will dictate the efficacy of all of your future rituals and spells. So, during the next year and a day of your training keep meditation somewhere in your routine.

Method

Sit or stand comfortably. Stretch a little to get a feel of your body. This doesn't have to be too complex of a step. Simply tilt your head side to side to sort of loosen up your neck muscles. Lift your arms above your head and stretch, etc. The purpose here is just to give yourself an awareness of your body.

Close your eyes, and get comfortable. Once you're comfortable, your body will begin to relax. When this happens, begin a count. Start at any number and count forwards, backwards, in sequence, pairs, or multiples. It's really up to you. I start at 9, and count in 9's until I lose count. 9, 18, 27, 36, 45, and so on. Once I lose count, I start at 8 and count in 8's until I lose count. Then 7, then 6, then 5, then 4, and so on. Eventually, the rest of my mind that wants to think about other things quiets. The trouble is, in the beginning you'll realize that your mind has quieted, and this will arouse thoughts of what to do next. That's ok. It's a normal part of this process. Learning to reach a peaceful state of mind takes practice in our world. For now, the purpose is just to begin the habit. However you choose to count should fit what makes you comfortable. If you want to start at 100 and count backwards, or even 10, is your choice. You could even imaging sheep jumping over a fence, or leaves falling off of a tree. Method here is personal, and should suit you.

Do this every day in some quiet and safe setting. The process of reaching a quiet mind is different for everyone, and there is no standard amount of time in which this will take. Be patient with the process, and work on it. Success will not be achieved on the first try, nor will your success be linear. You may succeed in quieting your mind, only to fail at it the next day. This is a process that will end up taking you one step forward just to yank you back three steps later. As frustrating as it is, this is completely normal because this is a process. Just remember that, for now, the goal is to establish a habit not perfect a skill.

DEFINITIONS

I know, I know. Any idiot with half a brain knows that the Glossary is always located at the back of the book. Well, this isn't a Glossary. It's a short list of definitions that you needed for the previous chapter and will need for the next. This is meant to be a workbook and an informational piece for the absolute beginner. There are new words and phrases that you're coming across, and you need to see the definition of these words as they apply to Wicca and Witchcraft when they come up. The incorrect attribution of definitions to these words can cause confusion later so I'm giving them to you now. I would challenge you to also search these terms out on your own, and define them in your own way.

Wicca- A nature oriented religion having rituals and practices derived from pre-Christian religious beliefs and typically incorporating modern Witchcraft.

Wicca is also a contemporary Pagan new religious movement. It was developed in England during the first half of the 20th century and was introduced to the public in 1954 by Gerald Gardner. Wicca draws upon a diverse set of ancient pagan and 20th century hermetic motifs for its theological structure and ritual practices.

Witchcraft- The art or practices of a Witch; sorcery; magic; Magical influence; Withchery

Religion- A set of beliefs concerning the cause, nature, and purpose of the universe usually involving devotional and ritual observances and often containing a moral code governing the conduct of human affairs.

Tradition- The transmission of customs or beliefs from generation to generation, or the fact of being passed on in this way.

In Wicca, a Tradition is a separate sect or denomination. There are various Traditions in Wicca, and all are valid.

Coven- A gathering or connection of witches. A group of thirteen is sometimes preferred, but the size of any given coven will depend upon its members.

Novice- An individual who has entered into the path of learning the ways of the Witch and/or Wicca and is still within their "one year and a day" course of study.

Initiation- Formal admission or acceptance into a coven. For the solitary practitioner, initiation can involve personal ritual customized for the solitaire. It is highly recommended that novices spend the traditional "Year and a Day" in a structured course of study for the discipline necessary to the craft.

Journey- Passage or progress from one stage to another

Phallus- An image or representation of the male reproductive organ

Wheel of the Year - An annual cycle of seasonal festivals observed by many modern Pagans. It ultimately consists of 8 festivals, although many traditions officially recognize 4, 6 or all 8. This varies and will depend on the ideas held within the tradition. The 8 festivals are Samhain, Yule, Imbolc, Ostara, Beltane, Midsummer, Lughnasadh, and Mabon. These 8 festivals make up the 4 solstices, and 4 equinoxes. The Wheel of the Year also contains 13 Esbats, which are lunar celebrations.
As you research the Wheel of the Year, Sabbats and Esbats will become clearer to you.

Pagan- A member of a religious, spiritual, or cultural community based on the worship of nature or the earth

Great Rite- A form of sex magick that includes either ritual sexual intercourse or a ritual symbolic representation of sexual intercourse. Most often performed by the High Priestess and High Priest.

Triple Goddess- Frequently described as the Maiden, Mother, and Crone of the Goddess. Each stage symbolizes both a separate stage in the life of women, and the phases of the moon. Each aspect rules over a different realm and for different reasons. As you research Goddess and Pantheons, you will develop a deeper understanding of this. For now, this basic definition should suffice.

Lord and Lady- The Horned God and Triple Goddess of equal standing with neither standing subservient to the other.

Horned God- He represents the male part of the Wicca's duo-theistic theological system. He is associated with nature, wilderness, sexuality, hunting, and the life cycle.

A Brief History

Now that we've covered what Wicca is and what Wicca is not, and the difference between Wicca and Witchcraft, let's talk history. To fully understand the journey you're on, you should understand its origins.

As I said before, Wicca has no central authority or religious text. Its core principles were outlined by a British Civil Servant name Gerald Gardner in the 1940's and 1950's, and by an unattributed poem titled the "Wiccan Rede." After England repealed its last Witchcraft laws in 1951 Gerald Gardner made the existence of his coven public knowledge.

Now let me be clear about another **FACT.** This will piss a lot of people off, but it needs to be made crystal clear. The truth is that Wicca, as a religion, was started by a dirty old man. Gerald Gardner was, among other things, a lunatic and a sexual predator. It's true that when you get to the Wheel of the Year you are going to see several correlations between Wiccan Holidays, and Christian Holidays. If you dig through history books, you will find that Christianity developed many of its holy days and their celebrations in such a way as to streamline conversion from primitive pagan religions to the faith of God. In the early days, however, many Christians faced persecution so this may have started as a way for early Christians to practice their faith without being found out. On the other hand, we Neo-Pagans have done something very similar, and for nearly the same reason when it comes to persecution, not conversion. When a Wiccan or other Pagan says that Such-and-Such holiday was stolen from the Pagans for conversion purposes, be weary. Some of that is true, and history bears out this fact. However, some Pagans are so bitter to Christians, and other Zoroastrian's, that they really believe this to be the fact of Every holy day, and they believe it with hate in their heart. Still, no matter what way you look at it, Gerald Gardner was a fucking lunatic. He lied about many things, including his qualifications, however, <u>that does not diminish the path we walk</u>. Keep these two things in mind as you move forward.

All Wiccan Traditions are direct branches from the Gardnerian Tradition, or they're branches of those branches. It all leads back to him. Unless you believe his story about his initiation, in which case, Wicca may well be a resurgence of a religion protected and passed down in secret through the Witch Burning Years.

No matter what you make of that, keep it in mind. Don't go around touting pride in the man without fully understanding this. Gerald Gardner didn't coin the word "Wicca." His terminology was "The Craft of the Wise." There is no real evidence that he ever really used the word "Wicca." By the way, "Wicca" is the gender male word for Witch. "Wicce" would be the gender female word for Witch. In addition, The Great Rite was initially intended as a form of ritual rape. A High Priest would name the next High Priestess, then in her gratitude, she would spread her legs for the High Priest, and he would ceremoniously fuck her to enliven a charge within the circle. The named woman would then become the High Priestess. Once she reached a certain age, she was expected to step aside for a younger, more beautiful replacement named by the same High Priest. Essentially, it was yet another religion that venerated the phallus, and denigrated the Female Divine, turning us women into whores.

I may not be happy about the beginnings here, but unlike Christianity where the followers decided that the triple Goddess would be the Virgin, Mother, and Whore, in Wicca, practitioners, thankfully, decided that this would not work. Because of splintering factions, and new formations, we can be thankful that Wicca doesn't belittle women. Instead, we have equal duality of the Lord and Lady whereby neither rules the other.

Exercise 3

Take the time to complete this exercise before moving forward. I know. You think you already know this history. Right...? Wrong...

Objective: Complete a search of each of the figures listed below, then give 1000 words for each person. Note the individual's history, age, date of birth, date of death when applicable, his or her contribution to Wicca, any contributions he or she made to society at large, any books he or she wrote and published, and his or her general views on Wicca. Anything else is extra brownie points, especially if you find out something interesting. Do not rely on Wiccan only websites. Many of them will give a false light on these figures. You're searching for the truth here. Keep that in mind.

Task 3.1

Witchcraft and Witches dot com have detailed histories of some of these figures, but mostly just use your brain. If you get the feeling that the information is too flowery, or watered down it probably is. Find at least three sources for each, and make sure that one of them is an independent resource not skewed to the Wiccan cause. This will give you a true picture of Wicca and Witchcraft as it began and how it has evolved.

Also, remember, that beginnings dictate neither the true quality nor importance of anything. This should take effort and a fair amount of time.

Aleister Crowley	Alex Sanders
Alex Winfield	Alice Walker
Carol Queen	Charles Caldwell
Deborah Lipp	Dion Fortune
Doreen Valiente	Gavin Bone
Gerina Dunwich	Granny Boswell
Helena Blavatsky	Janet Farran
Laurie Cabot	MacGregor Mathers
Margaret Murray	Margot Adler
Maxine Sanders	Patrick McCollum
Paul Beyerl	Phyllis Cabot
Raymond Buckland	Scott Cunningham
Silver Ravenwolf	Sybil Leek
Vivian Crowley	Zsuzsanna Budapest

Also research:

New Forest Coven

JUST A FEW TRADITIONS

Within Wicca there are many Traditions. Each Tradition has its own set of views, and all are different in some way. Although these Traditions are different, you should remember they are all valid. Remember that what works for one may not work for another.

Gardnerian Wicca

After England repealed its final remaining witchcraft laws in 1951 Gerald Gardner was one of the first to go public about his practice of Witchcraft. Because of his candidness he quickly became a figurehead of the Wiccan Religion. Gerald Gardner is seen as the founder of Wicca, and as such, Gardnerian Wiccan is seen as the Tradition from which all other Wiccan Traditions have branched off. Gardnerian Wicca is deeply delved into nature, colorful rituals, and it deliberately challenges the conventional religions and society as a whole. Individuals must be initiated by the coven and cannot initiate themselves. There is a structured degree system in which neophytes learn the craft. As a whole, this particular Tradition is secretive and its members generally don't share rituals and practices with outsiders.

Alexandrian Wicca

Alex Sanders who dubbed himself the "King" of witches founded this particular tradition in the 1960's. Much of this Tradition is based off of its parent Tradition, Gardnerian Wicca. However, Alexandrians tend to place more emphasis on ceremonial magic and includes some Judeo-Christian elements. As with GW, Alexandrian Wiccans must be initiated.

Seax Wicca

Also called Saxon Wicca was founded by Raymond Buckland in 1973 in the U.S. Buckland was originally a follower of Gardner but he moved to the U.S. in 1962 and gradually moved his coven away from the Gardnerian Tradition. Covens decide for themselves whether they want to work skyclad, or robe, and witches can be initiated either by the coven or by self-study.

Georgian

George Patters founded the Georgian Church in Bakersfield, California in 1970. This Tradition draws from Gardnerian and Alexandrian Wicca, among other elements.

Celtic or Druidic Wicca

Practitioners of this Tradition look to ancient Celtic and Druidic deities and beliefs with an emphasis on the magical healing powers of plants and minerals, and the prospects of gnomes, fairies, and other elemental spirits. Many of the rituals tend to be derived from Gardnerian practices with the main difference being its stress on the elements, nature, and the ancient ones. I should note that almost nothing is truly known about actual ancient Druidic practices.

Other Traditions that you could, and should, research include Blue Star Wicca, Black Forest Clan, Discordianism, Eclectic Wicca, Solitaires, and Dianic Wicca. Each of these Traditions has been impacted by their predecessors, and continues to influence Wicca and its teachings.

YOUR FIRST STEPS

By now, you've very likely read many other books on Wicca and Witchcraft and you've probably, against wiser advice, jumped into rituals, and works (spell casting). We've all done it. The lure of magical practices is too enticing. We just want to try it for the first time so bad.

Either way, you've come across the phrase "Book of Shadows." This chapter is going to discuss what a 'Book of Shadows' is and how to construct one.

First of all, a Book of Shadows (BoS) is your private book of works, rites, and thoughts. It should include basic information on the Wheel of the Year, and the Lord and Lady. It should also include any thoughts and feelings you experience during your journey. Most importantly, it will contain all of your future spells and rituals.

You can build one on your own. I did. I had a leather folio that used to have one of those calendars that could be taken out so another one could be slipped into the pocket. I built my BoS and keep it in that folio. As I create works, or design rites, I add in pages as needed. The pages are folded, stitch bound, and glued just like an old book. One of the benefits of having created my own BoS is that if I need to add in pages, I can simply disassemble the section and add in the pages I want. I've built the whole thing so I'm familiar with its work. A down fall of this is that it can be time consuming, and difficult to start. Despite the highly personalized nature of my BoS this method is not realistic for everyone. If, however, this method does appeal to you, simply search "Bullet Point Journal." You should find some interesting and instructive lessons on how to make one.

A second, and much easier, way to start a Book of Shadows is to purchase a journal that you keep specifically for this purpose.

A third option, if you like the idea of adding and subtracting pages and pieces as needed but don't want to build your own platform, is to assemble a binder or folder of all of your thoughts, spells, and rituals. You could add in folders and tabs for research, and for works as needed.

It's important to remember that this is not a date book nor is it a journal. This is **not** something that you should work on and then discard. Your BoS will be highly charged with your included works and your personal energy. Throwing this away or losing it could become catastrophic to your physical or emotional self. A BoS, especially for the solitary practitioner, should never be handled by or shared with someone who expresses disdain for your works. Within a Coven, the BoS is often built and shared collectively. For the solitary practitioner, keep your BoS to yourself. What works for you may not work for someone else, and in fact may cause harm to them. This is a tool, and a method of keeping a personal record. It is yours, and as such is highly personal.

I realize that many Witches share their spells in books online. I advise against this, and I won't use those spells. However, they can be useful as a general guiding post to give a new initiate some basic information and an idea of the overall layout of a work or ritual. The rites used for Sabbats and Esbats are something of a different story, however, because in the end we're celebrating or marking the same event in time. Use these published works as a guiding post only, be weary of the Witch that would draw you into performing baneful magick, and keep in mind the Law of Three.

Exercise 4

Task 4.1

After assembling your Book of Shadows, or deciding on the general layout, add in a section for "Thoughts During Meditation." Place a mark for everyday you've taken the time to be still and meditate for at least one minute. Your new challenge over the next month is to expand on that time. As you stretch your limits during meditation, keep a note of your experiences. At the end of the month, you'll read over your past months notes.

Task 4.2

Mark this page and come back to answer the following questions at the end of the next month.

Question 4.1

After reading over the past months notes, what, if anything, did you notice?

Question 4.2

How can you improve your meditation sessions?

Question 4.3

Have you had any sessions where you've successfully quieted your mind?

Question 4.4

What was the experience of returning after those sessions?

THE WHEEL OF THE YEAR

During the year we celebrate 8 Festivals. Because time is circular, not linear, a major part of some of these festivals is 'the return.'

The year starts on October 31 with Samhain. This is the time of year when the veil between this world and the spirit realm is thin enough for us to commune with our ancestors. We celebrate the cycle of life, death, and rebirth. The earth has gone dormant and has begun her slumber cycle through the harsh winter months. We are celebrating to remember that she will eventually awaken, and also that we will soon be reunited in the spirit world with loved ones that have preceded us.

Yule is a time for us to gather with still living loved ones, and celebrate their life, our life, and the shared love. Yule is celebrated between December 20 and December 23. Some traditions practice Yule all three days, while some people will recognize it on one specific day. Either way, it's a time for love, and the celebration of community and family.

Around about February 2nd we're all tired of the bitter cold, or otherwise contrary weather of winter. This is when we celebrate Imbolc to remind us that spring is around the corner. The sun is a little brighter, the days are a little warmer, and the return of life is around the corner.

The Spring Equinox, Ostara, occurs between March 20 and March 23. At this point Spring has arrived, and the ground is giddy with excitement as lilies and other early spring flowers have begun to sprout up.

For Beltane, May 1, April showers have lent the need of the earth to begin giving rise to crops and other life. Beltane, or May Day, is a celebration of fertility.

By Litha, The Summer Solstice between June 20 and June 23, gardens are blooming, and summer is full steam ahead. Litha honors the longest day of the year and as such the focus of Litha is on the Sun and its cycles.

Lammas, or Lughnasadh, is the time to finally reap what we have sown throughout this year. August 1 brings in the first harvest, and we celebrate the fruits of our labor.

Mabon, or the Autumn Equinox, is the mid-harvest festival. On or around September 21, this is a time for Wiccans to Give Thanks. We accept that the life of the year has passed, and the earth will soon enter her dormancy. The warmth is behind us, and cold lies ahead.

If you were looking for details on rituals and spells during these festivals I'm sorry to disappoint. You are here to learn, and part of learning is to find some of this information on your own. If you want spells and magic, then you're in the wrong place. I don't mean that you're reading the wrong book. I mean that if all you care about is spells, and magic, then you're not far enough along in your journey for such things.

Exercise 5

Task 5.1

Research each of the Great Festivals. Completing your research will give you an introduction into various Gods and Goddesses, and archetypes. It will also give you a basic idea of what is achieved during any rituals that may be carried out on such holidays.

Task 5.2

Name and describe an archetype associated with each festival. Give 250 words.

Task 5.3

Describe what we celebrate during each festival. Give 750 words for each festival.

Question 5.1

Are there any festival gatherings scheduled for your area?

What are they?

Where are they located?

When are these festival gatherings scheduled?

Who are the hosts for these gatherings?

Task 5.4

Design and Draw your very own Wheel of the Year Calendar.

Task 5.5

Associate a stone, color, archetype, and ritual for each festival.

Exercise 6

Task 6.1

Now that you're getting your toes into rituals and celebrations repeat after me.

"I am not alone. I am not alone. There is a community out there that will help me. There is a community of kind hearted souls eager to meet me, and welcome me."

Finding and gaining initiation into a coven can be very difficult. It's not like we advertise open slots in our covens in the want-ads. To find a coven you have to network, and find yourself invited into it. This is not a bad thing. This is a good thing. Many coven members are closer to each other than they are to their families. Many Wiccans are not out of the closet, and this is because many of us still face persecution in the wake of an outing. So we tend to guard ourselves.

However, if you find that you wish to practice as a solitaire, then you are still not alone.

Either way, there are many online Wiccan communities. Witch Vox is a great one, and so is the community Wicca page on Google Plus. There are regional and national Facebook groups. It is helpful to find a community, or three, and join in the conversation. You will learn so much. Go ahead give it a try.

If you don't want your family to find out... No sweat. Sign up for a second e-mail account with Google (Gmail). Once you have a g-mail account, you have a Google Plus account and the best part is that you can sign up with a pseudonym. The best groups that I've found are on Google Plus- just search "Wicca" within the G+ community platform. We share stories, experiences, festival rituals, simple spells, conversation, and art.

Just like with any online community, however, be careful. There is no truly safe place online and as always you should abide basic internet community safety. Don't share your personal information with anyone, or your family's personal information. Remain guarded.

UNDERSTANDING BASIC TENET'S

The following are the guide posts used in Wiccan practice and in Witchcraft Magick. Read each one and answer the questions at the end of the next chapter.

Wiccan Reed

Bide ye the Wiccan Laws ye must, in perfect love and perfect trust.

Live and let live, fairly take and fairly give.

Cast the Circle thrice about to keep the evil spirits out.

To bind the spell every time, let the spell be spake in rhyme.

Soft of eye and light of touch speak ye little, and listen much

Deosil go by Waxing Moon, Sing and Dance the Wiccan Rune

Widdershins go when the Moon doth Wane, and the werewolf howls by the dread wolfs bane

When the Lady's Moon is new, kiss thy hand to Her times two.

When the Moon Rides at Her peak, your heart's desire seek

Heed the North Wind's mighty gale, lock the door and trim the sail

When the Wind comes from the South, Love will kiss thee on thy mouth.

When the Wind blows from the East, expect the new and set the feast.

When the West wind blows o'er thee, departed spirits restless be.

Nine woods 'neath the Cauldron go, burn them quick and burn them slow.

Elder be the Lady's tree, burn it nor or cursed ye'll be

When the Wheel begins to turn, let the Beltane Fires Burn

When the Wheel has turned a Yule, light the Log and let the Horned One rule

Heed ye flower, bush and tree, by the Lady Blessed Be

Where the rippling waters go, cast a stone and truth ye'll know

When ye are in dire need, hearken not to others' greed.

With the fool no season spend, or be counted as his friend

Merry meet and merry part bright the cheeks and warm the heart
When Misfortune is enow, wear the blue star on thy brow
True in love ever be, unless thy lover's false to thee
Eight words the Wiccan Rede fulfill, an ye harm none, do what ye will.

The Witch's Creed

Hear now the word of the Witches, the secrets we hid in the night,
When dark was our destiny's pathway, That now we bring forth in the light.

Mysterious Water and Fire, The Earth and the wide-ranging Air,
By hidden Quintessence we know Them, and we will keep silent and dare.

The birth and rebirth of all Nature, the passing of Winter and Spring,
We share with the life Universal, rejoice in the Magickal Ring

Four times in the year the Great Sabbat, returns, and the Witches are seen,
At Lammas and Candelas dancing, on May Eve and old Halloween

When daytime and nighttime are equal, when sun is at greatest and least,
The four lesser Sabbats are summoned, again Witches gather in feast.

Thirteen silver moons in a year are, thirteen is the Covens array,
Thirteen times at Esbat make merry, for each golden year and a day.

The power has passed down the ages, each time between woman and man
Each century unto the other, ere times and the ages began.

When drawn is the Magickal circle, by sword or athame of power,
Its compass between two worlds lies, in the land of shades of that hour.

Our world has no right to know it, and the world beyond will tell naught,
The oldest of Gods are invoked there; the great work of Magick is wrought.

For two are the mystical pillars, that stand at the gate of the shrine,
And two are the powers of Nature, the forms and the forces divine.

And do what thou wilt be the challenge, so be it in love that harms none,
For this is the only commandment, By Magick of old be it done.

Eight words the Witches Rede fulfill:
An it Harm none, Do what Thou Wilt.

The Law of the Power

Written by Scott Cunningham

The Power shall not be used to bring harm, to injure or control others. But if the need arises, the Power shall be used to protect your life or the lives of others.

The Power is used only as need dictates.

The Power can be used for your own gain as long as by doing so you harm none.

It is unwise to accept money for use of the Power, for it quickly controls its taker. Be not as those of other religions.

Use not the Power for prideful gain, for such cheapens the mysteries of Wicca and magick.

Ever remember that the Power is the sacred gift of the Goddess and God, and should never be misused or abused.

And this is the law of the Power.

The Law

We are of the Old Ways, among those who walk with the Goddess and God and receive Their love.

Keep the Sabbats and Esbats to the best of your abilities, for to do otherwise is to lessen your connection with the Goddess and God.

Harm none. This, the oldest law, is not open to interpretation or change.

Shed not blood in ritual; the Goddess and God need not blood to be duly worshipped.

Those of our ways are kind to all creatures, for hurtful thoughts are quiet draining and aren't worth the loss of energy.

Misery is self-created; so, too, is joy, so create joy and disdain misery and unhappiness. And this is within your power. So harm not.

Teach only what you know, to the best of your ability, to those students who you choose, but teach not to those who would use your instructions for destruction or control. Also, teach not to boost pride, forever remember: She who teaches out of love shall be enfolded in the arms of the Goddess and God.

Ever remember that if you would be of our way, keep the law close to your heart, for it is the nature of the Wicca to keep the Law.

If ever the need arises, any law may be changed or discarded, and new laws written to replace them, so long as the new laws don't break the oldest law of all: Harm None.

Blessings of the Goddess and God on us all.

Charge of the Goddess

Listen to the words of the Great Mother, who was of old also called among men Artemis, Astarte, Diane, Melusine, Aphrodite, Cerridwen, Diana, Arianrhod, Bride, and by many other names.

At mine altars the youth of Lacedemon in Sparta made due sacrifice. Whenever ye have need of anything, once in the month, and better be it when the moon is full or new, then ye shall assemble in some secret place and adore the spirit of me, Queen of all Witcheries.

There shall ye assemble, ye who are fain to learn all sorcery, yet have not won its deepest secrets: To these will I teach things that are yet unknown.

And ye shall be free from slavery. And as a sign that ye be really free, ye shall be sky clad in your rites. And ye shall dance; sing; feast; make music, and love, all in my presence, for mine is the ecstasy of the spirit, and mine also is joy on earth for my law is love unto all beings.

Keep pure your highest idea; strive ever toward it. Let naught stop you or turn you aside,

Mine is the Secret that opens upon the door of youth, and mine is the cup of the wine of life, the cauldron of Cerridwen, which is the Holy Grail of Immortality.

I am the gracious goddess who gives the gift of joy unto the heart of man. Upon earth I give the knowledge of the spirit eternal. And beyond death I give peace and freedom, and reunion with those who have gone before, nor do I demand sacrifice, for behold, I am the Mother of all living, and my love is poured out upon the earth.

Hear ye the words of the Star Goddess: She in the dust of whose feet are the hosts of heaven, whose body encircleth the universe.

I who am the beauty of the green earth, the white moon amongst the stars, the mystery of the waters, and the desire of the heart of man call unto thy soul. Arise and come unto me.

For I am the soul of nature who giveth life to the universe; from me all things proceed, and unto me all things must return, and before my face, beloved of gods and men, thine inmost divine self shall be enfolded in the rapture of the infinite. Let my worship be within the heart that rejoiceth, for, behold, all acts of love and pleasure are my rituals. Therefore, let there be beauty and strength, power and compassion, honor and humility, mirth and reverence within you.

And thou who thinkest to seek for me: know thy seeking and yearning shall avail thee not, unless thou know the mystery, that if that which thou seek thou finds not within thee, thou wilt never find it without thee.

For behold, I have been with thee from the beginning, and I am that which is attained at the end of desire.

I seek the Crown of Wisdom and understanding that Might and Mercy in balance bring Beauty. Victory and glory find their foundation in Summerland.

The 13 Wiccan Principles

1: We practice rites to attune ourselves with the natural rhythm of life forces marked by the phases of the Moon and the seasonal Quarters and Cross Quarters.

2: We recognize that our intelligence gives us a unique responsibility toward our environment. We seek to live in harmony with Nature, in ecological balance offering fulfillment and consciousness within an evolutionary concept.

3: We acknowledge a depth of power far greater than that apparent to the average person. Because it is far greater than ordinary, it is sometimes called supernatural, but we see it as lying within that which is naturally potential to all.

4: We conceive of the Creative Power in the universe as manifesting through polarity ~as masculine and feminine~ and that this same Creative Power lies in all people, and functions through the interaction of the masculine and feminine. We value neither above the other, knowing each to be supportive to each other. We value sex as pleasure, as the symbol and embodiment of life, and as one of the sources of energies used in magickal practice and religious worship.

5: We recognize both outer worlds and inner, or psychological, worlds sometimes known as the Spiritual World, the Collective Unconscious, Inner Planes, etc. ~and we see in the interaction of these two dimensions the basis for paranormal phenomena and magickal exercises. We neglect neither dimension for the other, seeing both as necessary for our fulfillment.

6: We do not recognize any authoritarian hierarchy, but do honor those who teach, respect those who share their greater knowledge and wisdom, and acknowledge those who have courageously given of themselves in leadership.

7: We see religion, magick, and wisdom in living as being united in the way one views the world and lives within it ~a world view and philosophy of life which we identify as Witchcraft~ The Wiccan Way.

8: Calling oneself "Witch" does not make a Witch, but neither does heredity itself, not the collecting of titles, degrees, and initiations. A Witch seeks to control the forces within her/himself that make life possible in order to live wisely and well without harm to others and in harmony with Nature.

9: We believe in the affirmation and fulfillment of life in a continuation of evolution and development of consciousness giving meaning to the Universe we know and our personal role within it.

10: Our only animosity towards Christianity, or towards any other religion or philosophy of life, is to the extent that its institutions have claimed to be "the only way", and have sought to deny freedom to others and to suppress other ways of religious practice and belief.

11: As American {Or World-Wide!} Witches, we are not threatened by debates on the history of the Craft, the origins of various terms, the legitimacy of various aspects of different traditions. We are concerned with our present and our future.

12: We do not accept the concept of absolute evil, nor do we worship any entity known as Satan or the Devil, as defined by the Christian tradition. We do not seek power through the sufferings of others, nor accept that personal benefit can be derived only by denial to another.

13: We believe that we should seek within Nature that which is contributory to our health and well-being.

Wiccan Rune
Written by Doreen Valiente

Darksome night and shining moon
Harken to the Witches Rune
East then South, West then North
Here come I to call thee forth.

By all the powers of land and sea
Be obedient unto me.
Wand and pentacle, cup and sword
Harken ye unto my word

Cords and censor, scourge and knife
Waken all ye into life
Powers of the witch's blade
Come ye as the charge is made.

Queen of heaven, field and dell
Send your aid unto this spell.
Horned hunter of the night
Work my will by magick rite.

By all the might of moon and sun
As I do will, it shall be done
By all the powers of land and sea
As I say, so mote it be.

By all the might of Moon and Sun,
As I do will, it shall be done.

REVIEWING THE BASIC TENET'S

Now that you've had a chance to read the Wiccan Reed, The Witch's Creed, the Wiccan Rune, The Law of Power, the Charge of the Goddess, and The 13 Wiccan Principles lets cover each one in some more detail.

The Wiccan Rede can be broken down into 5 separate components that have been poetically assembled for better understanding. Those 5 separate components work to explain one main principal. "An it harm none, do what ye will." This is open to neither interpretation nor excuse. The most basic, and fundamental rule of Wicca is "Harm None." Does this make us pacifists? Nope. Not in the slightest. You are allowed to defend yourself by whatever means necessary when you are in physical, emotional, or spiritual danger.

One way to look at this is as an hypocrisy. If someone is attempting to harm you, you have a choice. Defend yourself, or passively allow this harm to be done to you. If you defend yourself, harming your attacker may be unavoidable. On the other hand, if you allow yourself to be harmed, you are in effect harming yourself.

On the flip side of this, outright attacking someone proactively is not acceptable. It causes harm to the other person without also preventing harm to yourself. This includes physical, emotional, and spiritual harm. This is one of the reasons we Wiccans don't proselytize. Proselytizing effectively attacks someone else's existing belief system. Where many people are searching, those who are comfortable and happy with their beliefs should not be attacked. It may cause undue emotional harm should these attacks cause a crisis of faith. This is different than talking to someone, or answering questions posed to you by someone who is interested, curious, or searching. Actively seeking these people is a thing far removed from standing on a street corner yelling at sinners and heathens.

Another thing to consider is that many Wiccans view this as a rule to become Vegans. I do Not! As Wiccans, we recognize the world around us to be part of a cycle, and everything within that cycle is living. Eating plants, therefore, is still devouring the life of a component of our environment. Obtaining required sustenance is necessary to continue life. As long as you 'eat what you kill,' eating meat is acceptable. Overeating is not. If you are fat because you overeat, then you are causing continual harm because you are contributing to the consumer count that says we need more and more. We must consume more and more. If you overconsume then you are causing harm. This goes for anything; paper, sugar, soap, water, any resource…

The Five separate components within the Wiccan Rede are Morality, Spellworks, Premonitions, Instructions, and Festivals.

Morality:
"Live and let live, fairly take and fairly give."
"Soft of eye and light of touch, speak ye little, and listen much."
"Merry meet and merry part bright the cheeks and warm the heart."

If I were to say to you to live and let live, what would your inner response be to this statement? Basically this means exactly what it says. Live and let live. Walking around on a high horse telling others how to live, giving unsolicited advice at the wrong moment, or basically being any kind of know-it-all makes you a douche. Don't assume that because something works for you, it should be thus for everyone else around you.

"Speak ye little, and listen much." Shut-up and listen. In my professional industry we have something called 'Active Listening.' Because part of what I do is in sales, active listening involves listening to my prospective client, their objections, hopes and dreams so that I can respond and counter as to why my product is what they actually are looking for. One of the problems with active listening is that it's leaked out into society and people are so busy listening to each other just so they can respond and argue. Try listening to someone else, and hearing what that person is saying without thinking of a way to respond. Basically, sometimes we just need to shut-up and listen. Try practicing this from time to time. You'll notice at least two things. The first is that you'll hear more of what's going on around you. Your interpersonal relationships will grow, and you will find yourself more attune to your natural environment. The second is that by quieting your self-righteous opinions, you'll find meditating much easier as your mind will quieten easier as well.

"Merry meet and merry part" basically means that there is no reason to just pick a fight. If you meet someone new, give the situation the benefit of the doubt. You might make a new friend. Also, If you have a good relationship with somebody, don't go out of your way to sabotage it. As for complete strangers, there is no good reason to ever be a douche unless you're defending yourself. Leave any encounter better than it was when first initiated. This will transfer to spell works as well, but we'll get to that later.

Spellworks:
"Cast the Circle thrice about to keep the evil spirits out."
"To Bind the spell well every time, let the spell be spake in rhyme."
"Deosil go by Waxing Moon."
"Widdershins go when the Moon doth wane"
"When the Moon rides at her peak, Your heart's desire doth seek"
"Nine Woods 'neath the Cauldron Go, burn them quick and burn them slow."
"Elder be the Lady's tree, burn it not or cursed ye'll be."

We haven't covered rituals or spells yet. This will be addressed later in this series. I don't want to be responsible for any novices jumping into spells and rituals before first learning to control yourself during meditation, grounding, charging, and circle casting.

Premonitions:
"Heed the North Wind's mighty gale, lock the door and trim the sail."
"When the Wind comes from the South, Love will kiss thee on thy mouth."
"When the Wind blows from the East, expect the new and set the feast."
"When the West wind blows o'er thee, departed spirits restless be."

North, South, East, West... All four of the cardinal directions in which a wind can blow in from. This discusses the importance of each force, as well as a time of year associated with their feast. A basic understanding of the Wheel of the Year will explain this. If you completed Exercise 5 then you have the basic knowledge to understand this concept within the Wiccan Rede. If not, go back and complete that exercise at this time.

Instructional:
"When the Lady's Moon be new, kiss thy hand to Her times two."
"Where the rippling waters go, cast a stone and truth y'ell know."
"Heed ye flower, bush and tree, by the Lady Blessed Be."
"When ye are in dire need, hearken not to other's greed."
"When Misfortune is enow, wear the blue star on thy brow."

"When the Lady's Moon be new, kiss thy hand to Her times two." This instruction can have many meanings, but the most important one to keep in mind is that you're being told to remember your Goddess, and respect her. Also, don't allow yourself to be taken in by the greed of others. We are most susceptible to manipulation when we find ourselves in trouble. If you do find yourself in trouble then you know that you can turn to the Divine for comfort. At the very least, I find that meditation and yoga opens my mind to problem solving.

Exercise 7

Task 7.1

Re-read the Wiccan Rede with the previous chapter in mind.

Task 7.2

When you've re-read the Wiccan Rede you should take the time to meditate on what you've read. You know all of those short meditative sessions you've been doing. Those have been practice. By now, if you've followed my advice, you should have a comfortable area in which to meditate, and have a process for quieting your mind. After you've stilled yourself, consider what you've read, and see where your thoughts take you.

When you're done meditating, write your thoughts down. You'll want to come back to these later. There isn't a future assignment for this in this book, but as you progress in your journey you'll find that you want to revisit your thoughts during this time to see how you've progressed. This will help with that.

Exercise 8:

Task 8.1

I did this for you with the Wiccan Rede, now it's your turn. In your separate notebook that you no doubt already have, and have set up for these exercises, answer each of these questions. The base answers to all of these questions are found in the Wiccan Rede, the Witch's Creed, the Wiccan Rune, The Law of Power, the Charge of the Goddess, and 13 Wiccan Principles although some of the explanations are explained elsewhere in either this work book, or assigned research.

1. What secrets do Witch's keep?
2. What are the eight most important words in the Witch's Creed?
3. What is the relevance of 13?
4. What is that which a Wiccan seeks?
5. What is authoritarian hierarchy?
6. What does the Witch's Creed say about advertising your path to become a Wiccan?
7. Why is it a bad idea to read spell books others have published?
8. What is supernatural? (Not the T.V. show!)
9. What is a Wiccan's view on authoritarian hierarchy? Why?
10. Do Wiccan's worship satan or demons? Explain your answer.
11. Do Wiccan's seek power through the suffering of others? Explain your answer.
12. What are the seven main tools used in spell work? List and describe each one, and their purpose.
13. Describe the two dimensions, and their importance.
14. Please give a detailed description of each basis, and explain their importance.
15. List two ways in which The Power shall not be used.
16. How is misery self-created?
17. Can Power be used for your own gain? Explain your answer.
18. Explain what purchasing a spell book from anther Witch would accomplish for you, or how it might negatively impact your future work.
19. Do Wiccan's accept the concept of absolute evil? Explain your answer.
20. What are the four Great Sabbats?

21. Give an explanation for the purpose of the feast, and how we celebrate each of the Great Sabbats.
22. What is the one part of the Law that can never be changed?
23. How can happiness be self-created?
24. Why do we practice rites?
25. How does the Witch's Creed connect the ritual circle, and the Wheel of the Year?
26. What is the Creative Power, and how is it viewed by Wiccans?
27. What is the purpose of working sky clad?
28. What is our personal role within the Universe?
29. List and Explain each of the four relevancies of the number 13.
30. What is the basis of Balance in Magick, and Wicca?
31. What are the 8 characteristics of a true Wiccan?
32. Given the Wiccan's views expressed in the Wiccan Rede what is the one and only animosity that we, as a collective, hold for Christianity, Islam, and Judaism?
33. Why do we draw a circle for spells and rituals?
34. Is working sky clad optional?
35. What is the purpose of "Charging"?
36. What does a Witch seek to control?

Exercise 9:

Task 9.1

Write each of these three statement 100 times each. Do not try to do this in one sitting. Your hand will cramp, and then it will be me causing harm. Get your notebook, and write each one out in increments of five or ten, or so, a day until you've written each statement 100 times separately.

1. As Witches, and citizens of the Wiccan community, we are not threatened by debates on the history of the Craft, the origins of various terms, or the legitimacy of various aspects of different traditions. We are concerned with our present and our future.

2. I will not actively proselytize. I will respect the religious views of others, especially when they differ from my own views and opinions. I will not belittle or attempt to malign the different traditions within Wicca, or other Religions. I understand that there are many paths that we can follow, and all are relevant.

3. As a Wiccan, I will seek within Nature that which is contributory to my health and well-being. I will afflict no self-harm, and I will not seek to harm others through general actions, deeds, or specific craft works.

FINAL THOUGHTS

There is so much more that you need to know. In order to continue in your training keep a habit of meditating and reading each day of your journey. Also, please hold to a year and a day before you begin your initiation. You should have a full understanding of the basic workings of Wicca before you try anything advanced.

For magick, and before you try any spells, please read the following books. Most of them you will be able to find at a local library. All of them can be found on Amazon. Some of the information across these titles will be contradictory. Remember that this is alright. We accept the diversity of opinions in Wicca because what works for me may not work for you. After reading these titles you'll have a better understanding of charging and grounding and why this is important; casting a circle and why and how this should be done properly; the role of the guardian; a better understanding of the Lord and Lady; your sacred space and how to prepare it; your work tools; and the cardinal elements.

You should NEVER try a spell before you have mastered these skills. Without a full knowledge of what you are doing, you could do serious harm to yourself and to others.
Keep to your journey, and walk it soberly.

Guide for the Solitary Practitioner
Living Wicca
Earth Power
Earth, Fire, Wind and Water
Witchcraft Today
All By
Scott Cunningham

Overcoming Obstacles to Meditation
A short Guide
Andres Pelenur

Wicca for Beginners
A Guide to Real Wiccan Beliefs, Magic and Rituals
Gillian Nolan

Living Wicca Today
Wiccan and Pagan Holidays
Kardia Zoe

Encountering the Goddess
Vol 1 and 2
Sarai Posavec

Drawing Down The Moon
Margot Adler

Wicca- A Year and a Day
Timothy Roderick

Blessed Be.

Printed in Great Britain
by Amazon